© 2010 by Marilyn Spooner

All rights reserved. No part of this publication may be reproduced, stored in a retrieval system or transmitted, in any form or by any means, electronic, mechanical, photocopying, recording, or otherwise, without prior written permission from the publisher.

For information about purchasing a copy of this book, please contact:
Elaine Spooner, elainewrites3022@gmail.com
or
Barbara Riley, briley5@hotmail.com

Book Design by Carol O'Keefe		Published by Elaine Writes Media

Dedication

This Book is dedicated to:

Carl and Millie Spooner
Parker J. Spooner
Bertha Spooner Knapp

First, let me introduce myself. As this book title says, I'm **The Barn That Moved Away**, far away, from where I had stood for nearly one hundred years on a farm in New Hampshire to the island of Martha's Vineyard off the coast of Massachusetts.

What follows is the story of my remarkable journey.

My home, Maple Lane Farm, is named for the magnificent maple trees which line the road leading to an old-fashioned farmhouse and *me*.

The change of seasons meant my surroundings were never boring.

While I resemble barn friends in the neighborhood, it's my size and how I was built that make me unique.

Extra long and wide, I'm large enough inside my walls to hold an Olympic-size swimming pool, leaving plenty of space for cheering spectators (and one lonely owl).

As for how I'm built, it's a construction method known as post and beam. Vertical and horizontal beams, cut by hand from hardwood such as oak, are fastened together with wooden pegs, also hand-hewn. The result is a special type of framework that requires no support in the middle (creating plenty of empty space for that imaginary pool), yet keeps me straight and strong to withstand harsh New England weather and the passage of time.

What kind of lifestyle was it for me and Maple Lane Farm during our early years? Very different from that of today. Milking was done by hand. Horses pulled the plow, the harrow, which smoothed out the up-turned soil to make fields ready for planting, the rake, and a wagon to be filled with new-mown hay gathered up by pitchfork and stored in my spacious loft as winter feeding for cows waiting in the stable below.

It was 1939 when a new family purchased Maple Jane Farm. I was somewhat worried when I heard the news. What sort of family would it be? But when I saw the farmer, his wife, and two teen-aged children exploring the farm with obvious delight, I could tell they would truly appreciate my place on the farm and treat me with affection and respect.

I relished their pleasure in discovering the maple tree grove in a half-wooded pasture beyond one field. The family was thrilled to find that sap could be gathered to make their own maple syrup for their favorite Sunday morning pancake breakfasts.

How I often wished I could join them.

Hay smells of sweet clover as it fills my loft, but I consider it quite tasteless.

I often wonder why my Holstein tenants enjoy it so much!

As the new family settled in, it was even more satisfying to realize that the farmer believed in the old saying, a place for everything and everything in its place. I bragged to my friends how clean and spotless the entire farm was kept. Lawns were mowed, flower beds weeded, my floors swept each day, tools and farm equipment put back where they belonged after use. And the small white picket fence on the front lawn was painted every spring. By hand, mind you. A slow process. Spray painting had not been invented yet.

Thank goodness, the farmer's wife believed in that old saying as well. She wanted the large, white, green-trimmed farmhouse as neat and tidy as the farm itself.

To make sure, there was always a complete house cleaning from cellar to attic every spring and fall.

No dust bunnies frolicking under her beds!

I could tell, too, that the farmer's wife loved flowers, especially the old-fashioned red rambler rose climbing a trellis by her kitchen door.

Then there were the apple blossoms every spring from the small orchard behind the farmhouse. The farmer's wife's pies could win a blue ribbon and became special treats for family and friends.

On baking days, waves of that mouth-watering aroma drifted across the way between the kitchen and me. Delish!

How quickly time passed. Changes occurred. Farming became easier with the use of a milking machine. A tractor took the place of horses. Molly and Ned were retired to pasture. I could often spot them enjoying leisurely days of a well-earned rest from pulling a heavy hay wagon and plowing and harrowing long rows of corn and oats.

A mechanical baler now swept up the hay, tossing bales onto the back of a truck instead of a wagon. My loft was filled with tightly-packed bales instead of loose hay. Of course, the cows could care less how the hay was stored as long as they got their twice-a-day meals.

Eventually, however, it came time to once again sell Maple Lane Farm. It was purchased in 1969 by a family from Massachusetts. I was happy to see this new family loving the farm and working hard to keep it prosperous and well-cared for as others had before them. They also continued to be proud of me and my contribution to their farm's well-being.

When the farmer's wife left Maple Lane Farm and moved to town, she took her beloved rose bush with her. It was carefully replanted by the kitchen door of her new home. I got word years later that a granddaughter now lives in the house and lovingly cares for the old rose bush. It continues to bloom profusely every June.

Once again, the years sped by. It came time to give up farming due to low milk prices and hired help became hard to find. While the new owner's wife continued to live in the old farmhouse, Maple Lane Farm, including me, fell silent and pretty much deserted.

My loft remained empty. My stable had no cows waiting to be milked. The fields were only cut to keep them free of bushes and saplings. I was very sad and lonely. I missed the hustle and bustle of farm chores and feeling useful. I wondered if I would end up like so many of my barn friends, suffering the indignity of collapsing roofs and buckling walls. We thought of ourselves as neglected and unappreciated.

Then one day my world changed completely. A knock on the front door of the farmhouse brought the owner's wife hurrying to answer. She found a group of people standing on the porch. One man smiled at her and then politely asked, "Would you be willing to sell us your barn?"

What a surprise. They wanted just me not the farm. What did it mean? Quickly, I found out. The group represented the Martha's Vineyard Agricultural Society. Members had been searching for an old post and beam barn they could dismantle, ship to the Island and rebuild as an exhibit hall on their newly designed fairgrounds in West Tisbury. An annual harvest fair is a favorite late summer event and they needed a proper centerpiece.

In case you are unfamiliar with Martha's Vineyard, it is a roughly triangular shaped island just 7 miles off the coast of Massachusetts. It is named for the daughter of an early ship captain explorer. The vineyard part of its name refers to an abundance of wild grapes which once grew there.

Today, the Island is thickly settled, especially during summer months. Full-time residents and visitors enjoy the Island's beauty and sun-filled days and unique setting. I couldn't have been more pleased at the possibility of moving there.

The current owners hated to see me leave, of course. But with the farm no longer active, they had worried that their beloved barn would end up in ruins like so many of my friends. To say the least, I was very thankful the owner had the presence of mind to provide me with a useful life again. But I wasn't all that sure how such a deed could be accomplished.

I soon found out. On a rather blustery March day in 1993, Agricultural Society members and volunteers arrived at Maple Lane Farm.

Climbing out of trucks and a pickup or two, I could tell they were eager to begin the first steps in dismantling me for my journey to the Vineyard. It seemed pretty scary, and I couldn't be entirely sure I wouldn't end up like dear old Humpty Dumpty!

Fat, saucy snowflakes flirted with the workers. Sometimes I saw as many as seventeen people at once, climbing up ladders with ropes and pulleys to remove my roof, side walls and framework. As they labored, I felt so strange and confused. Here I was, beginning to lie in pieces on the ground, not my humongous self at all.

I was glad, however, to hear cheers and note high-fives from the workers on how well preserved my beams were. Those townspeople who came to watch the unusual proceedings joined in with congratulations and admiration for the efficiency and precision in the tagging and numbering of each post, beam and peg.

Of course, for me the entire experience was quite upsetting!

Five days later, trailer trucks and pickups left Maple Lane Farm with over 700 pieces of what was once a barn. Next stop, Woods Hole, Massachusetts, 220 miles away.

From there, it was a short ferry ride to Vineyard Haven. You can understand how nervous I was during this part of my journey. I had been standing on firm ground for nearly a century. Suddenly, I am riding over deep water, no land in sight. Thank goodness, the sea was calm that day. Imagine all my 700 pieces getting seasick!

The actual barn raising took place in 1994. Hundreds of volunteers showed up to raise my old beams, new walls, and roof. It was a very exciting time. So much so that the Barn Raising Ball held at the time became an annual event.

Donations of money and offers of help poured in to raise those pieces into place. I was indeed honored by everyone's devotion and willingness to help make sure I became a suitable exhibit hall. I looked forward to my transformation from red clapboard to brown cedar shingles, with a small annex built to serve as an entrance and space for Society meetings. A small cow weathervane placed on the roof provided a touch of New England countryside. I thought my new appearance definitely prepared me for whatever came my way on Martha's Vineyard.

Hundreds of visitors and residents wander through my open interior, admiring the colorful displays and me in my new role as an exhibit hall extraordinaire. I may not be a regular Yankee barn as when I stood on Maple Lane Farm, but as an exhibit hall on Martha's Vineyard, I am considered special, one of a kind.

During fair festivities, I am the center of attention with my spacious interior filled with displays of crafts, baked goods, canned fruits and vegetables, pickles, jams and jellies, flower arrangements, photography and artwork entries.

Several times a year, the Martha's Vineyard Agricultural Society allows weddings to take place in between exhibit hall events. While a few family weddings occurred on Maple Lane Farm, I only caught a brief glimpse of the bride and groom as they entered the old farmhouse for the ceremony. Now it is wonderful to actually witness the entire service as each of the couples in all their wedding finery repeat their I do's.

Memories of Maple Lane Farm continue to stay with me. But I am thankful to find myself useful again. And how nice to hear from Society members and residents saying, "We love our barn." My beams go all aflutter with pride.

To those who lived on Maple Lane Farm and remember me still, rest assured that I expect to be around for another one hundred years as a beloved landmark on Martha's Vineyard.

So, dear readers, come and visit the Island and me, especially during one of our annual Harvest Fairs. They're awesome!

www.ingramcontent.com/pod-product-compliance
Lightning Source LLC
Chambersburg PA
CBHW041649160426

43209CB00019B/1863